WHEN I GROW UP I WANT TO SHINE BRIGHT

This book belongs to:

Written and Illustrated by:

ALTHEA HURLOCK

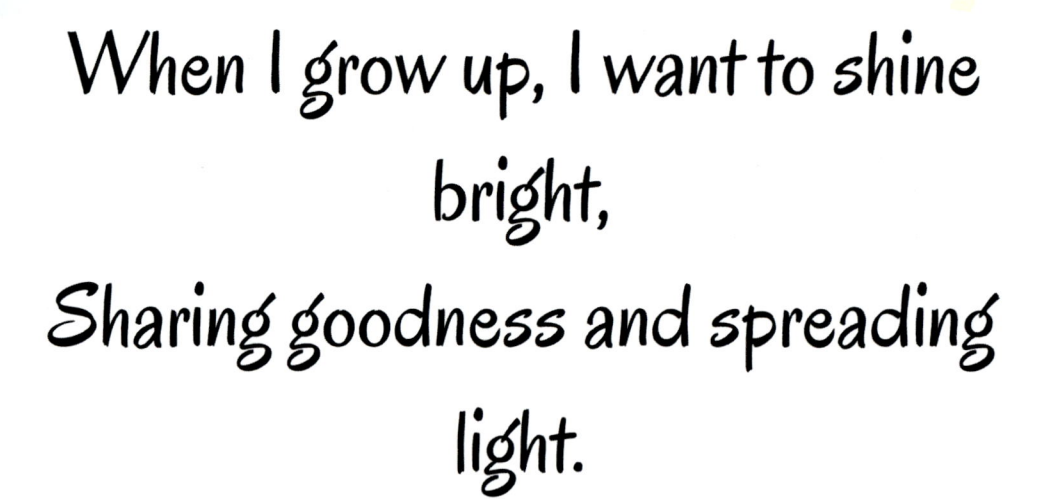

When I grow up, I want to shine bright,
Sharing goodness and spreading light.

I will be kind to everyone I greet,
with a warm smile and words soft and sweet.

Kindness creates bonds and brightens the skies, it brings joy to all and lights up our lives.

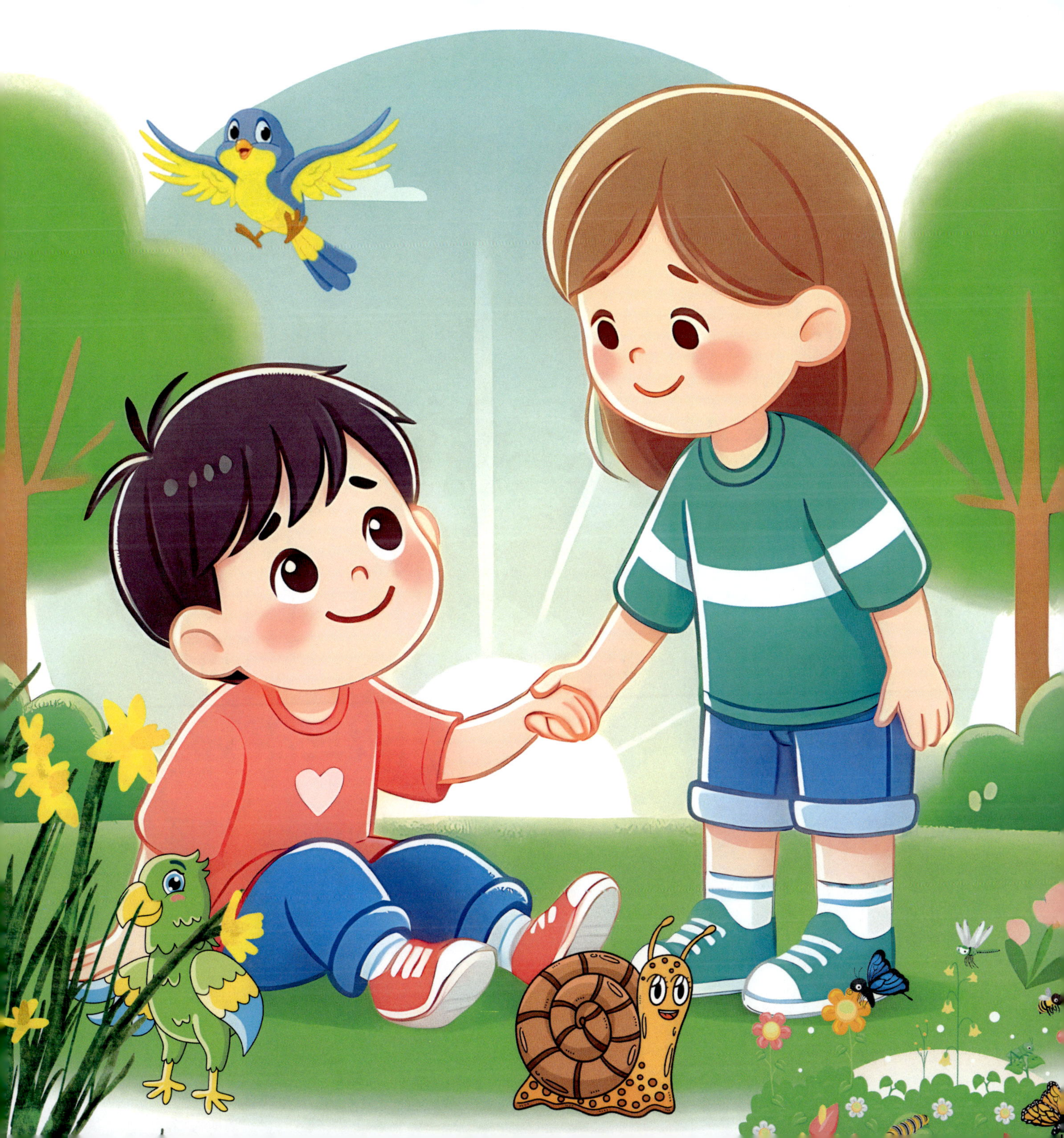

I will be honest and always tell the truth, even when it's tough, I know it's the right move.

Honesty builds trust and helps friends stay close, it reveals my true self and shows who I am most.

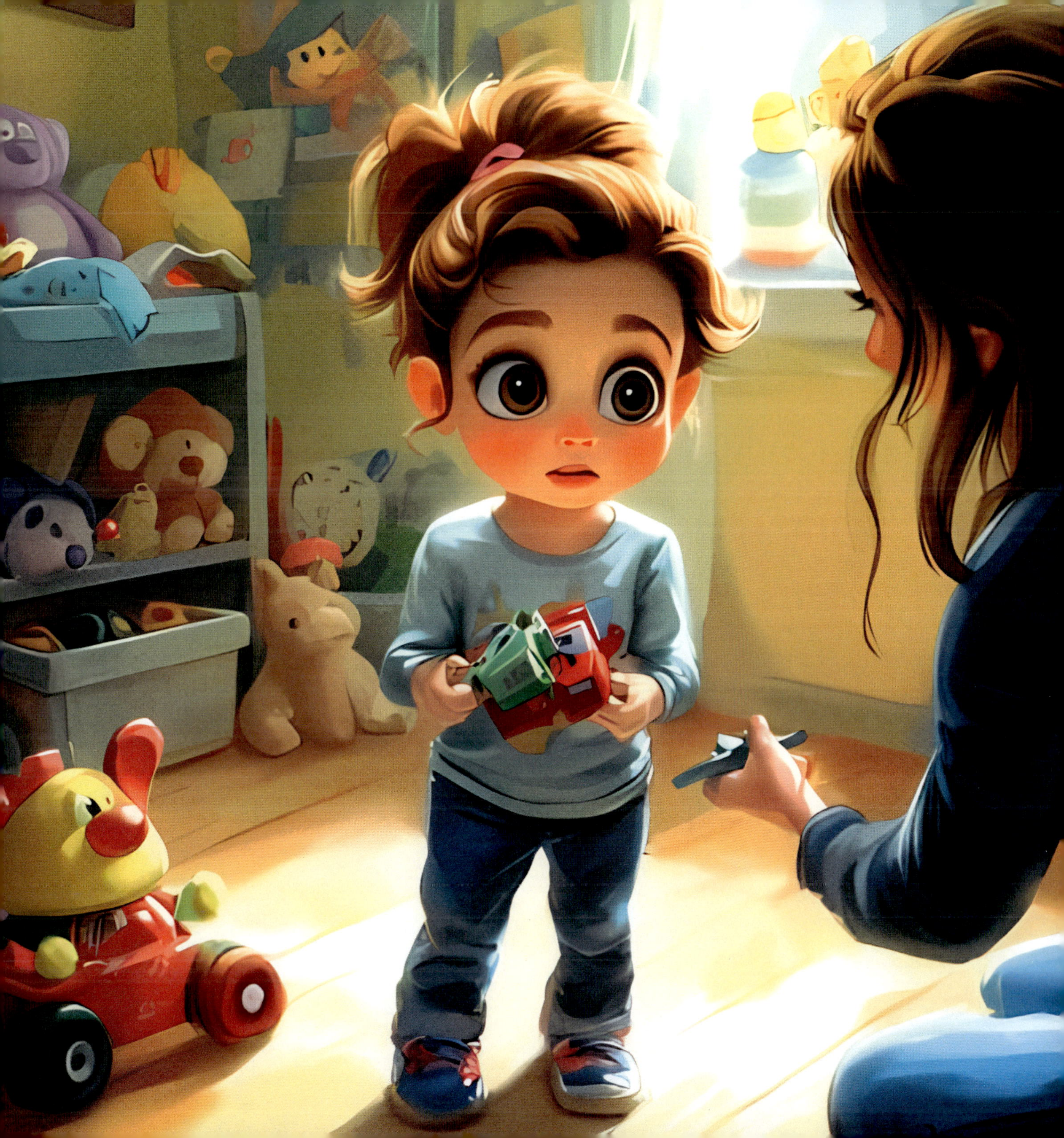

I will share with others and be kind every day, helping my friends in a thoughtful way.

Sharing makes sure everyone feels they belong, it spreads happiness and helps us stay strong.

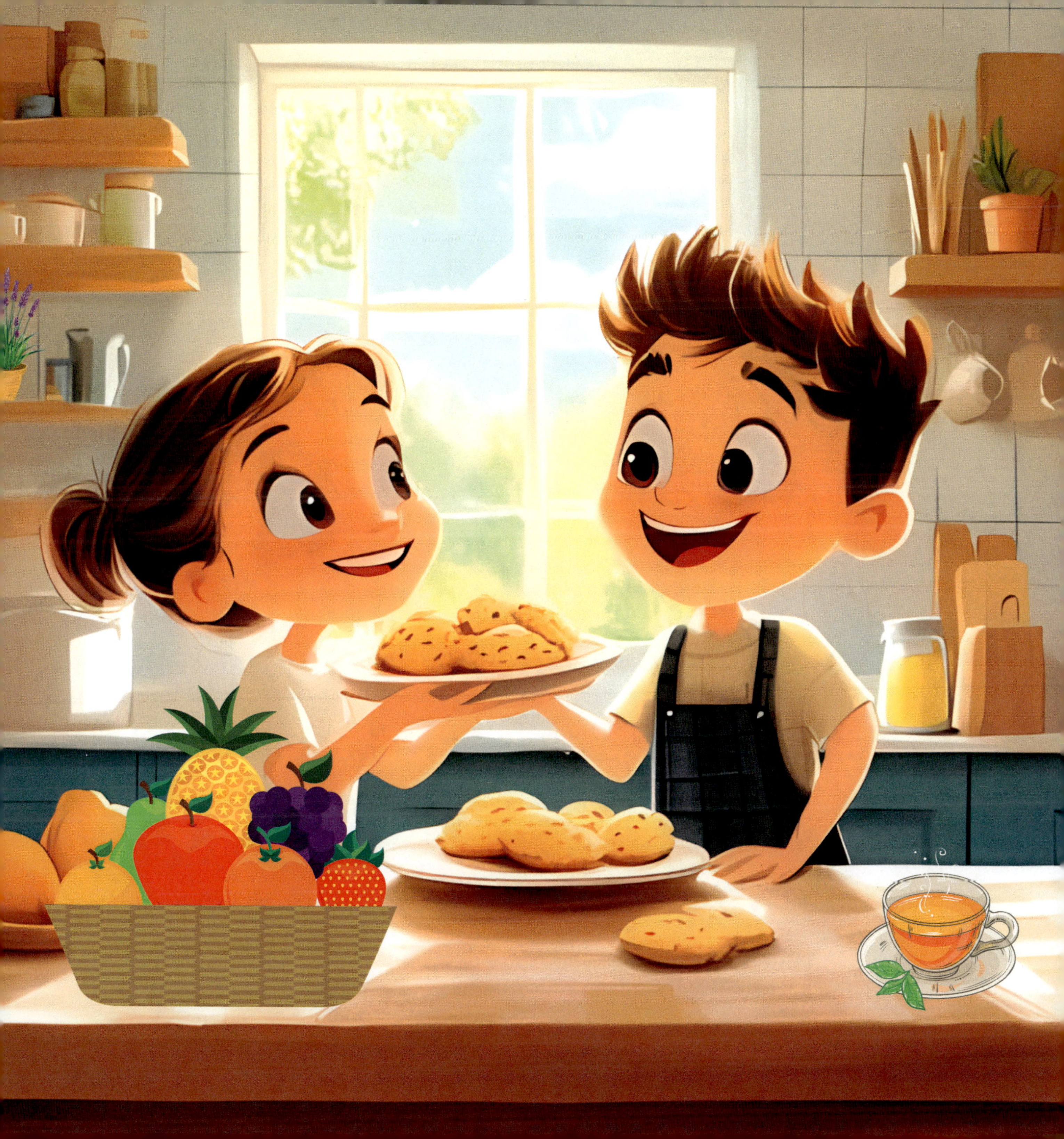

I will be patient and wait my turn,
good things come to those who learn.

Patience brings rewards when I don't rush,
It helps me enjoy things without a fuss.

ice-cream

I will have confidence and believe in me,
trying new things to see what I can be.

Confidence helps me reach for the sky,
It gives me the courage to always try.

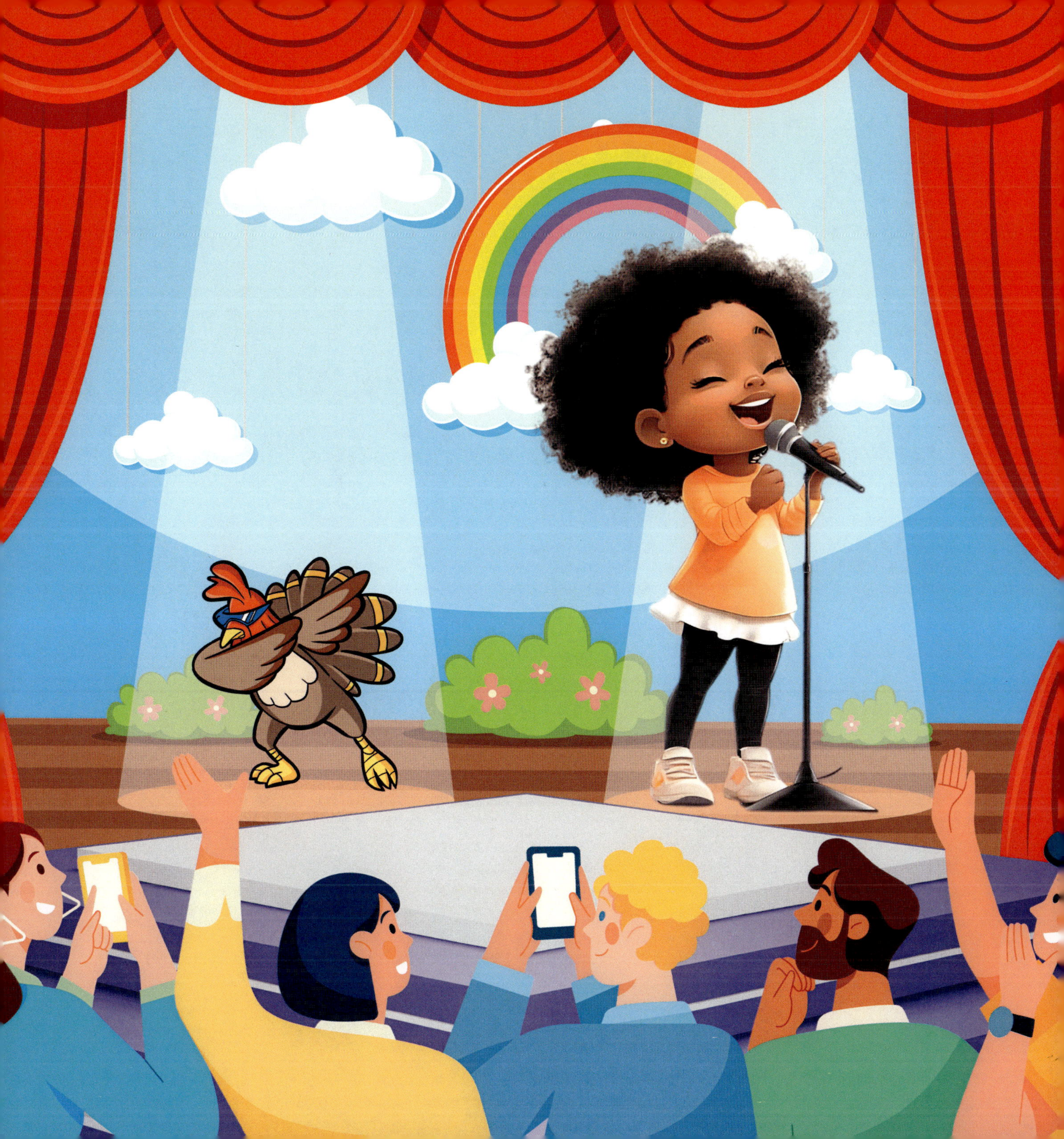

I will be respectful, listening with care, treating others kindly and always being fair.

Respect helps everyone feel valued and seen, It makes our world peaceful and keeps it serene.

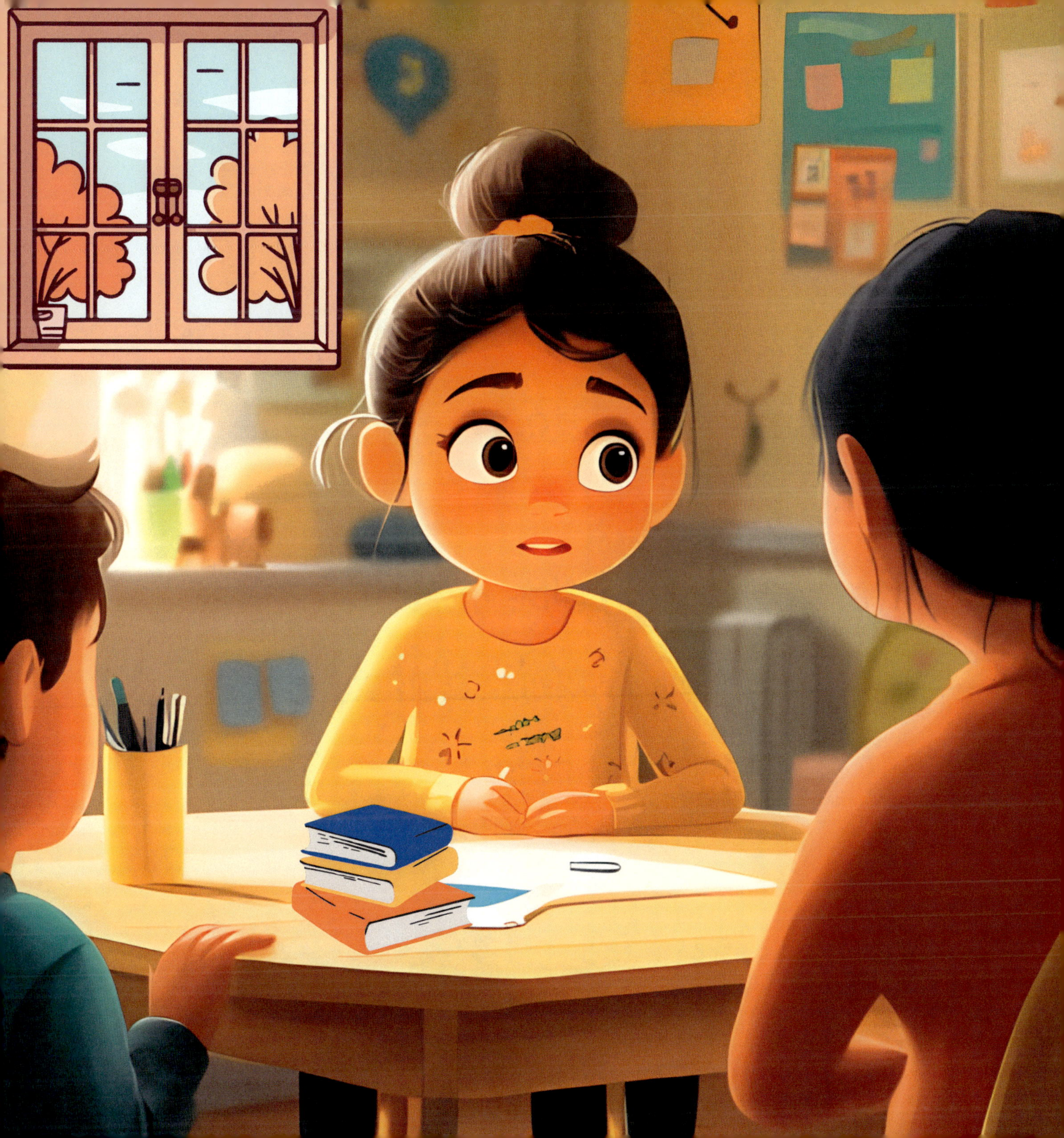

I will be responsible for all that I do, taking care of myself and my things too.

Responsibility helps me stay on track, It keeps me organized and helps me not slack.

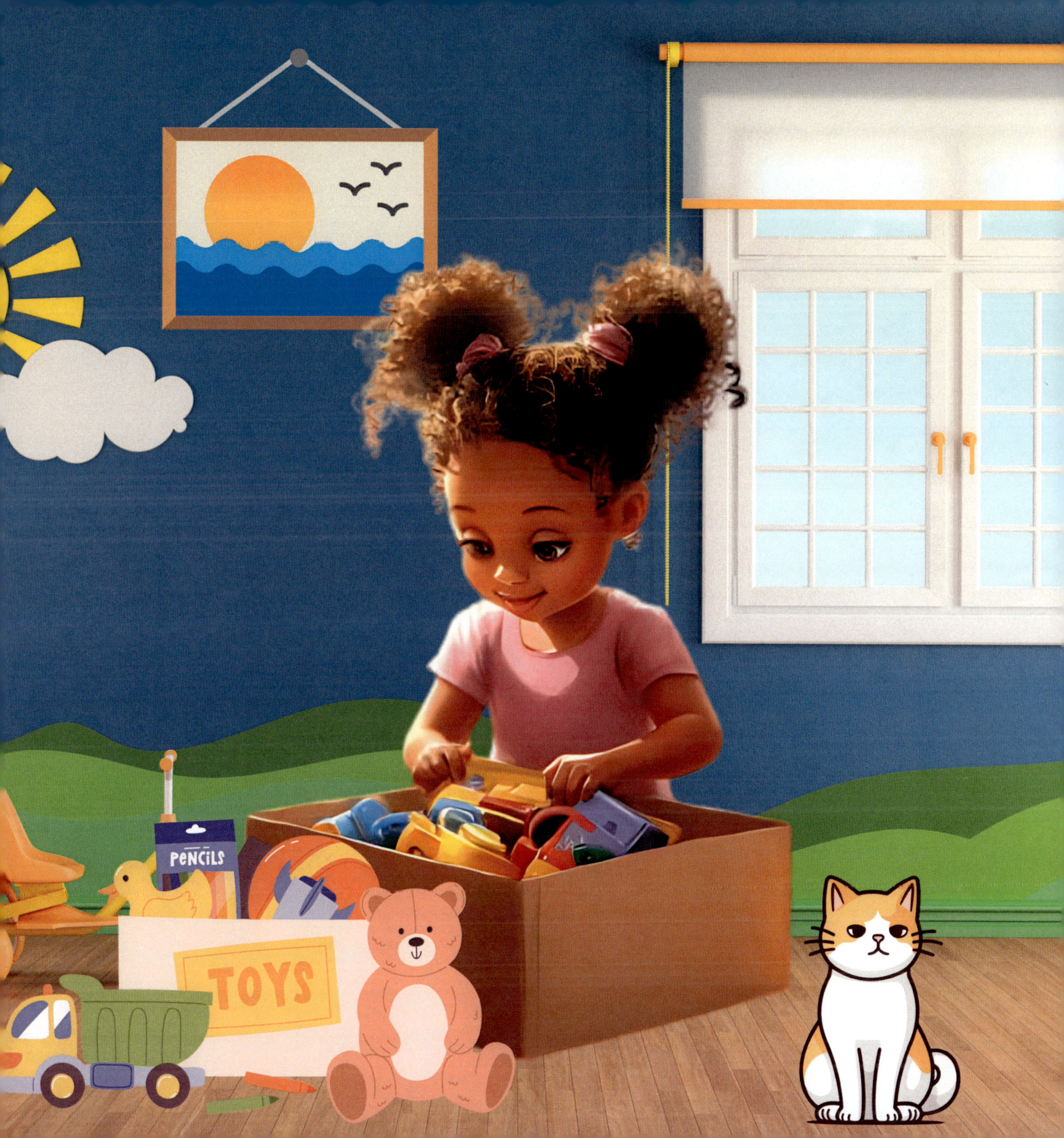
PENCILS
TOYS

I will practice gratitude and say, "Thank you," for all the good things I have and what's new.

Gratitude makes me happy and bright,
It helps me appreciate life's delight.

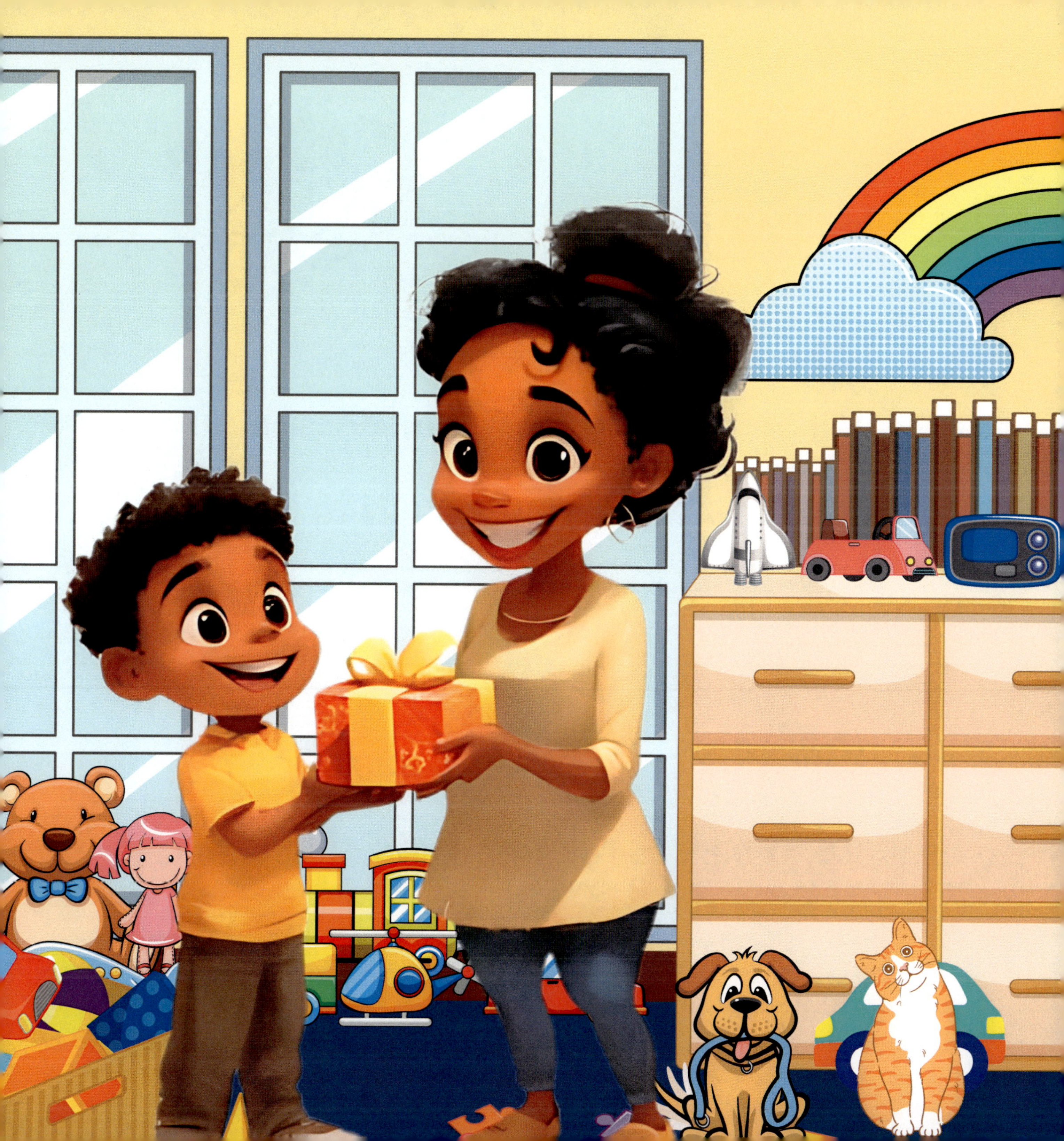

I will be full of empathy, understanding how you feel, offering a hand to help and to heal.

Empathy builds bonds and shows I care, It makes relationships strong and fair.

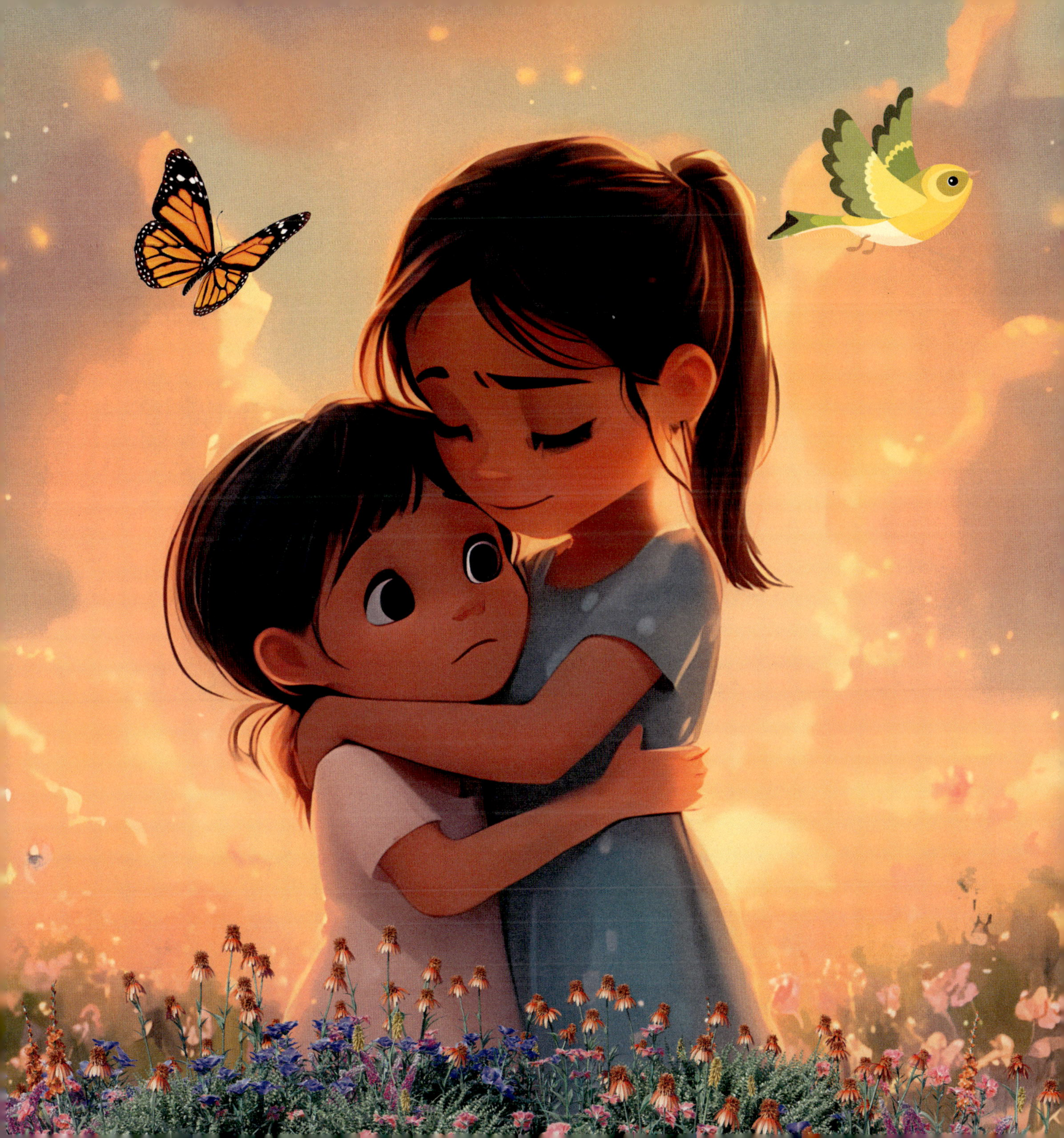

I will have perseverance, never giving up, even when it's tough, I will keep looking up.

Perseverance helps me push through the fight, It keeps me moving toward goals in sight.

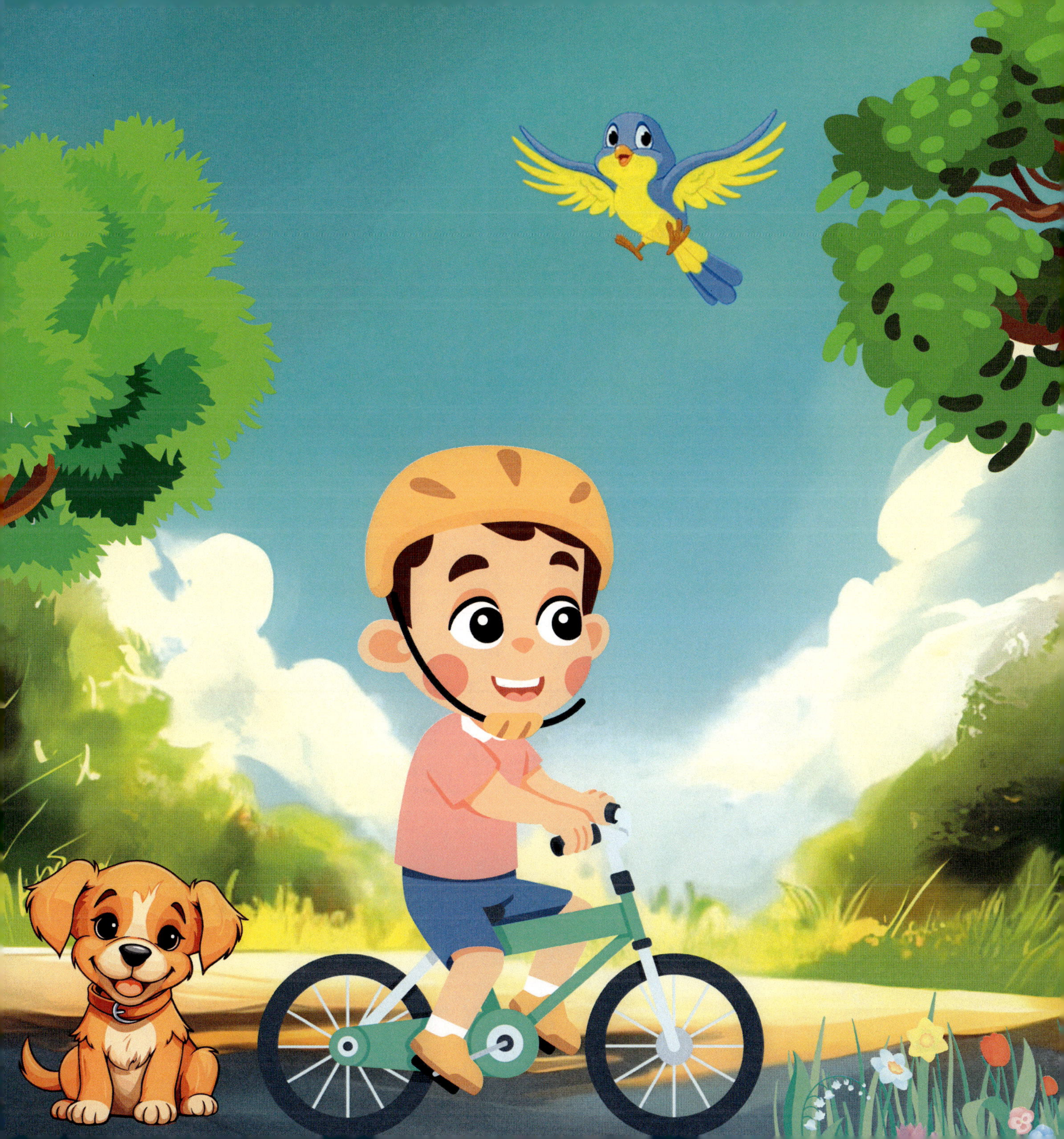

I will show compassion, caring for all, helping whenever I hear someone call.

Compassion makes the world a better place, It helps others feel love and grace.

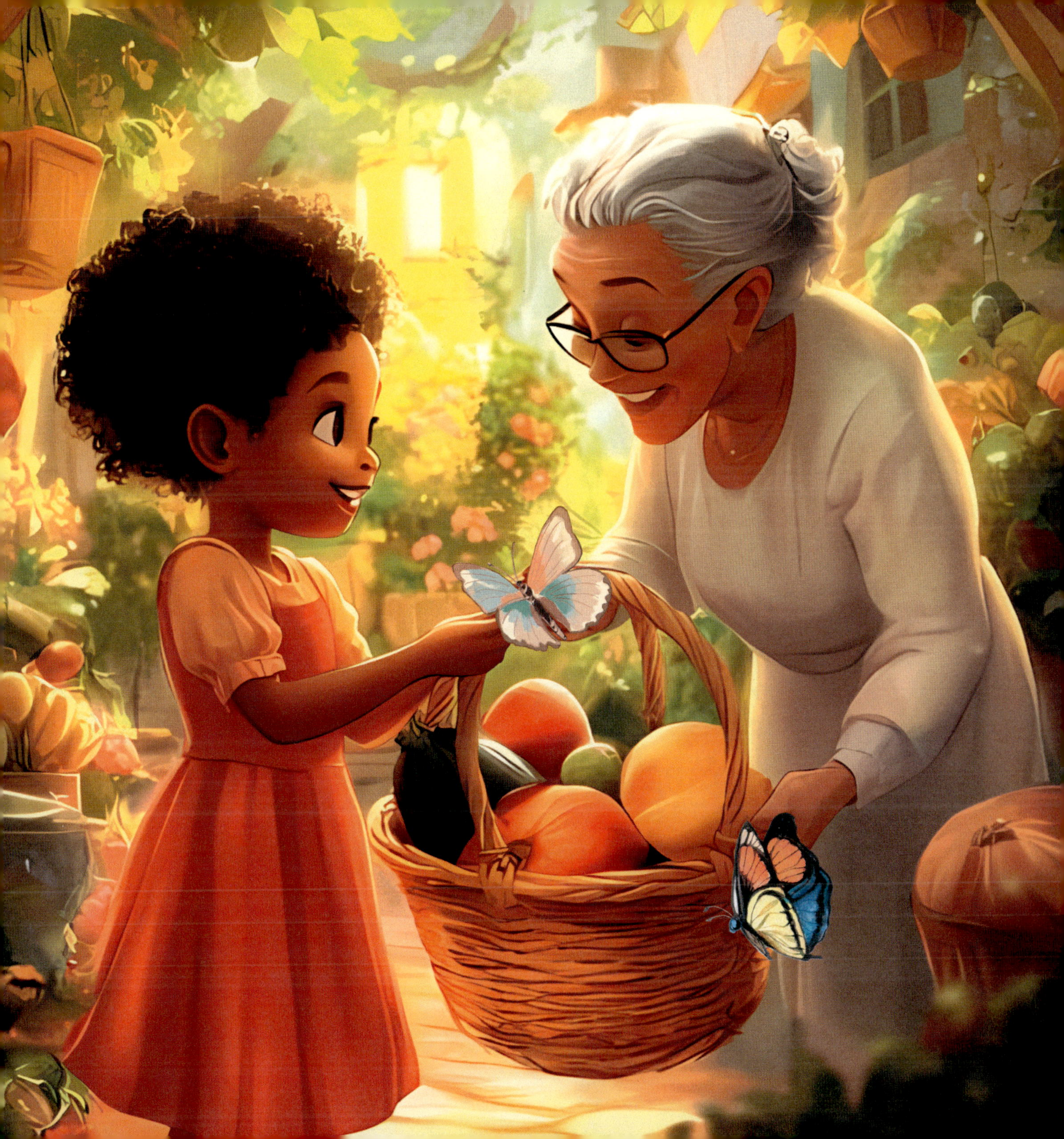

I will be thoughtful, considering what others need, helping them grow, letting kindness lead.

Thoughtfulness shows I care and understand, It makes life better and helps others feel grand.

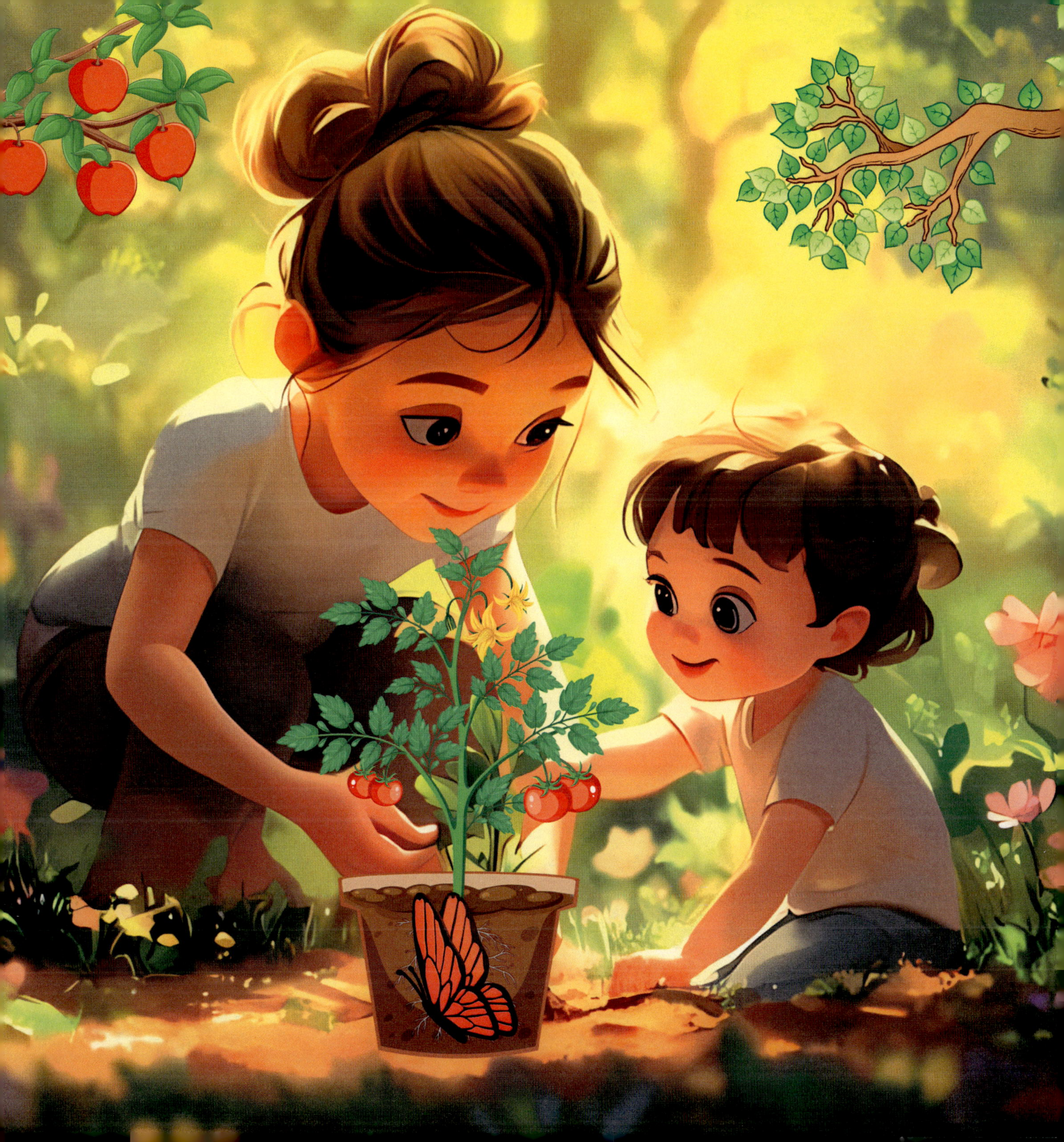

I will practice forgiveness, letting go of the past, mending hearts quickly, so joy will last.

Forgiveness helps me and others feel whole, it clears away pain and lightens the soul.

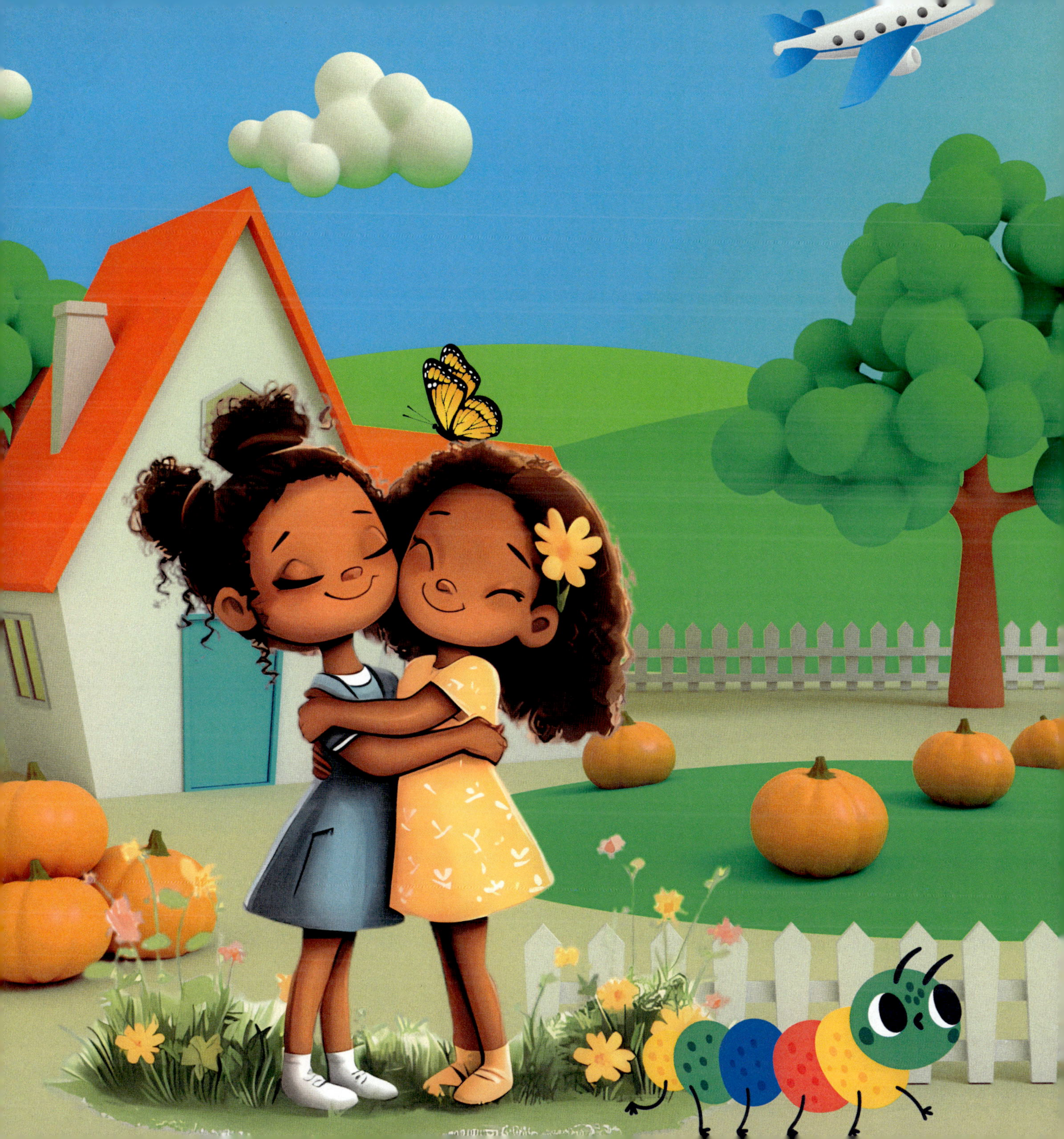

I will practice self-control, thinking before I act, making choices that keep me on the right track.

Self-control helps me make choices that are smart, It guides me to do right from the start.

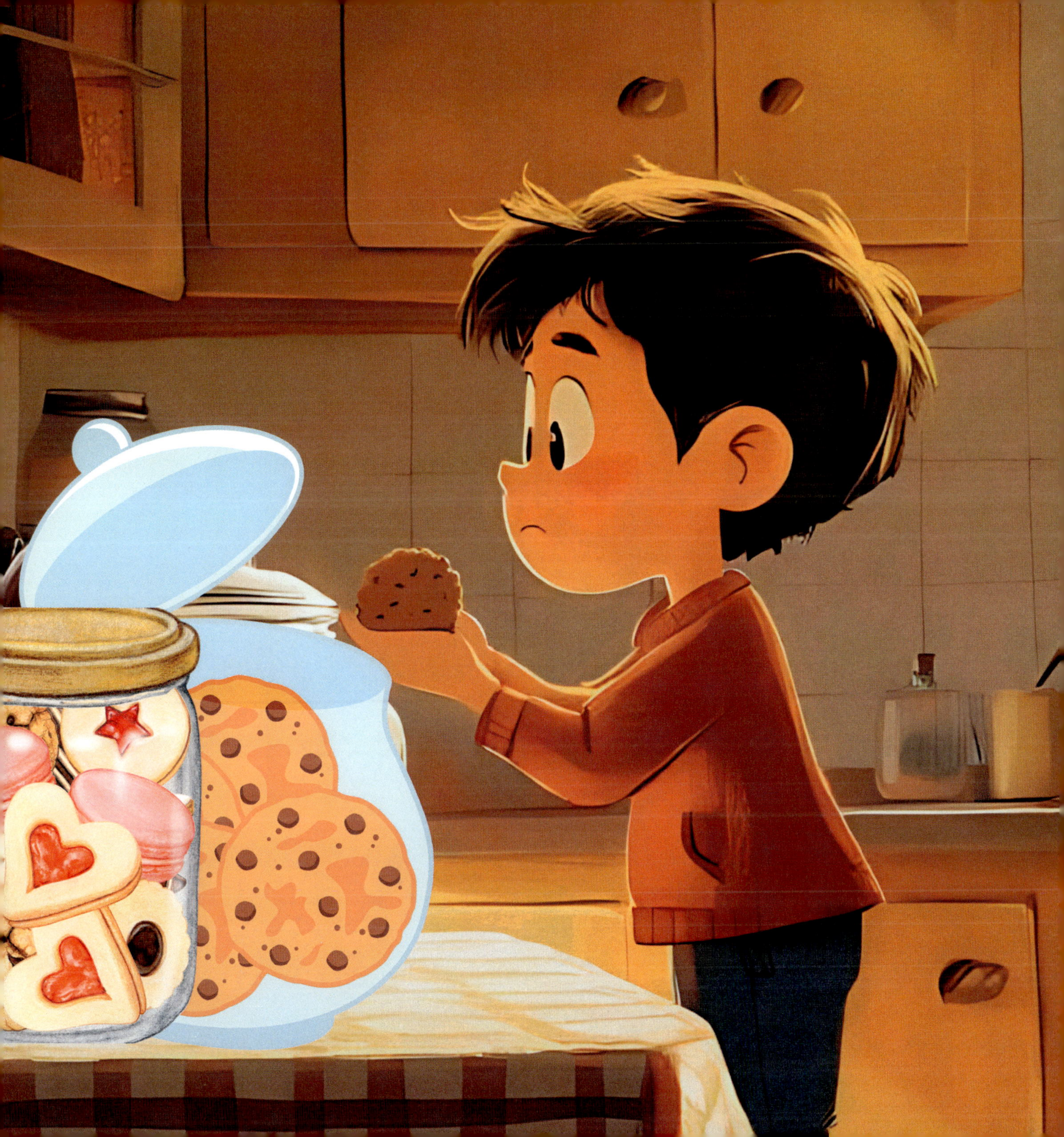

I will be trustworthy and keep my word, so everyone knows they can trust what they have heard.

Trustworthiness builds bonds that are strong, It shows I am reliable and where I belong.

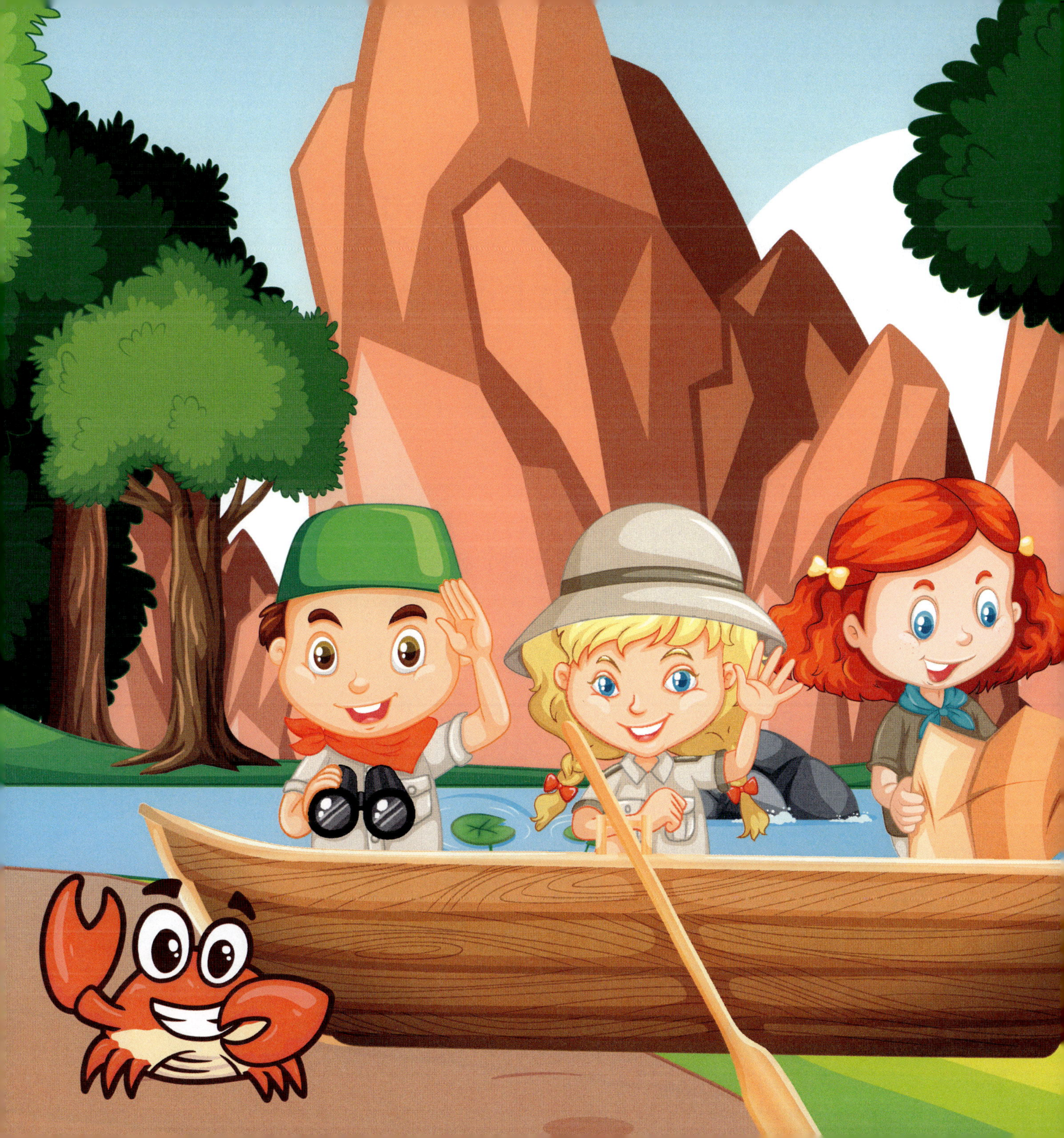

I will be humble, knowing I can grow, learning from mistakes and from others know.

Humility helps me stay grounded and wise, It opens my heart and helps me realize.

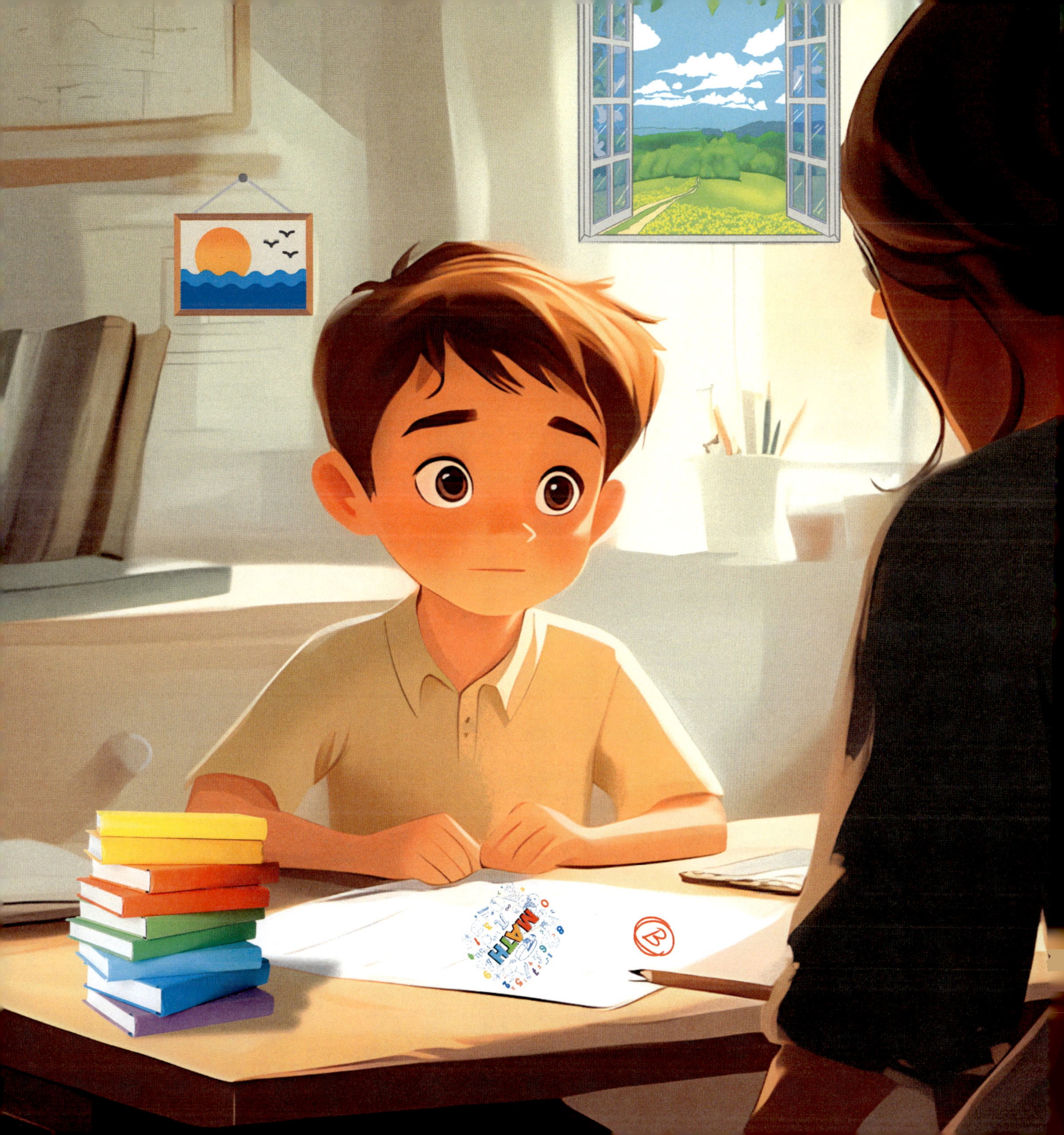
MATH
B

When I grow up, I will shine so bright,
Spreading goodness like stars in the night.
And with optimism, I will keep hope in my heart,
Believing tomorrow is a brand-new start.

Copyright © 2024 Althea Hurlock.
All rights reserved. No part of this publication may be reproduced or transmitted in any form or by any means without permission from the author.

Made in the USA
Las Vegas, NV
30 November 2024